M000040578

How to Make
an Examination
of Conscience

A Redemptorist Pastoral Publication

One Liguori Drive ▼ Liguori, MO 63057-9999

Imprimi Potest:
Thomas D. Picton, CSsR
Provincial, Denver Province
The Redemptorists

ISBN 978-0-7648-1682-6
Copyright © 2007, Liguori Publications
Printed in the United States of America
12 13 14 15 / 7 6 5 4

Liguori Publications, a nonprofit corporation, is an apostolate of the Redemptorists. To learn more about The Redemptorists, visit Redemptorists.com.

To order, call 800-325-9521
www.liguori.org

How to Make an
Examination of Conscience

Catholics are privileged to meet the Lord in the Eucharist and in other sacramental moments. This booklet will help you prepare to receive the sacrament of reconciliation (also known as confession) by helping you make a good examination of conscience. God's power and love are evident in this sacrament of forgiveness.

What Is an
Examination of Conscience?

An *examination of conscience* is a review of our life since our last confession, a tool to help us redirect our steps toward Jesus and away from anything or anyone who leads us away from God or God's kingdom.

As we review our life and acknowledge we have sinned, we hold up the Gospel as a mirror and try to see ourselves honestly, trying to identify what we have done wrong and looking for the root causes and motivations behind these poor choices. We open ourselves to the love of God, who is always ready to forgive us. We ready our spirit so God can accomplish his work in us. In sum, a good examination of conscience helps us reorient our life toward God, who *is* love, and to correct the actions, habits, attitudes, and motivations that are contrary to the teachings of the Gospel.

We believe God's power is most evident when he pardons us. God pardons us because he loves us and wants what is best for us. He takes the initiative to offer us forgiveness—but we must be ready to receive it in the sacrament of reconciliation.

Elements of a Good Examination of Conscience

A good examination of conscience helps us identify and address or correct harmful actions, habits, attitudes, and motivations. It is very important to define these words and behaviors before we make an examination:

a) For our purposes, an *action* is an isolated deed or occasion of sin. It may be a serious or light offense, but it is not continually repeated—for example, becoming angry with someone who arrives late, hurting someone once, or gossiping or cursing once. All of these actions are wrong and should be avoided, but one-time events should be recognized and treated as such.

b) A *vice* is an action that is repeated. It is a bad habit that is consciously or unconsciously part of a person's regular behavior. To be in a bad mood all the time, to constantly attack one or more persons, to continually lie: these are actions that have turned into vices, and they require serious attention. Sometimes a vice is rooted in an illness that requires professional medical treatment, such as dependence on or addiction to alcohol, drugs, gambling, and so forth.

c) Our attitudes and motivations, though often subconscious, exert a profound influence on our conscious decisions. Hatred, pride, racism, and materialism are just a few of the attitudes that negatively influence our choices and decisions. We must work hard to become aware of our own underlying attitudes and motivations so we can make choices and decisions that are conscious and free.

In the past, the Church instructed Catholics to mention the number of times they committed an offense. We are no longer asked to tally a particular sin unless it is very serious. Instead, we are urged to identify and confess the habits, attitudes, and motivations that influence our choices and result in sin so we can successfully improve our behavior.

Grace and Freedom

An examination of conscience is a personal exercise in which we look within our heart to recognize how we distance ourselves from God. At the same time, we must be open to God's grace. As God enters our heart through the Holy Spirit, we become more willing and able to live the Gospel in daily life. Our efforts would be fruitless without God's help, but God does not interfere with our free will. He acts only when we invite him into our lives and cooperate with his grace. Therefore, we need the Holy Spirit's help to make a good examination of conscience.

It is a paradox that we are most free when we acknowledge our dependence on God's grace: true freedom exists when we become the person God has created us to be, but our growth is dependent on God's help. One motivation for trying to live a good Christian life is to become an authentic, fully developed person. God helps us accomplish this goal when we use our intellect and will to follow Gospel values.

Our Actions Impact Society

Often we like to think our personal behavior has nothing to do with society's problems. The truth is we have an impact on society, and society has an impact on us. For instance, our style of dress is often influenced by the claims of the fashion industry; when we buy the latest styles, we drive consumer demand; increased consumer demand feeds the fashion industry.

Our individual actions also reinforce social behavior. For example, a chauvinistic father is likely to raise sons who will become chauvinists. A person who litters gives a bad example that others may follow. In short, every personal behavior has some effect on society.

It is important that our examination of conscience help us do what we need to do so we can become who we really want to be. We must reinforce positive values in our society by clearly opposing what is contrary to our personal values. We cannot justify ourselves with the excuse that "everybody does it." We must recognize that our personal actions always have repercussions and influence on others.

On one occasion a worker commented, "My salary is low and my boss exploits me. So, when I have the chance, I take some things from the office. It's not really stealing and, besides, my children will never know." This man is fooling himself. The unfair treatment by his boss is not justified, but neither is his stealing justified. Furthermore, he probably will not succeed in hiding his actions from his children, because everything we do is woven into the fabric of our life. Our decisions and actions color and shape our behavior.

God's Forgiveness Lasts Forever

When we participate in the sacrament of reconciliation, we needn't confess all the sins of the past; we need only confess the sins we have committed since our last confession. To reconfess past sins would be to doubt the reality of God's forgiveness. God is not like us. When God forgives, it is once and for all—complete and permanent.

Previous generations had a practice called *general confession.* At various points in their lives they would confess all the sins of the past—not because they needed to be forgiven again, but because they wanted to express their sorrow for the sins of their whole life. Such a practice, though not required, can be useful at certain turning points in one's life. But the truth still stands: *once God forgives our sins, no matter how serious, his forgiveness is total and lasts forever.*

Some situations require particular attention, for instance, persons with some type of physical or psychological dependency or other habitual sin. In such cases, an examination of conscience can help us recognize the seriousness of a particular repeated offense and the need to confess it once again with a sincere intention not to commit it again. In some situations, the priest may advise the penitent to seek professional help for his or her problem or to fulfill other specific conditions to receive absolution. But even then, the sacrament of reconciliation is meant to be a healing experience in conjunction with necessary and appropriate professional therapy.

Why Make an Examination of Conscience?

- To enjoy once again a healthy optimism about life, because God gives us the grace to make a fresh start.
- To enjoy harmony with family and friends, because our actions and attitudes form the basis of human relationships
- To awaken to the fact that we inhabit the earth, a creation of God, which has been given to us.
- To humbly recognize the parts of our life where we need to grow and improve.
- To move in the direction of freedom. Being free does not mean doing whatever we want

to do, but choosing to do what God invites us to do. This is true freedom.
• To enjoy living the supreme value that guides all of our actions: Love.

After making a thorough examination of conscience and our confession, we feel lighter. A good confession can dissolve the feelings of guilt that consume our energy and prevent us from becoming healthy, happy people.

Three Models

Saint Augustine said, "Love and do what you will." By this he meant that if our lives are full of the true love that comes from God, all our actions will be good. But few of us have achieved this level of love and purity. We need help identifying the actions, vices, attitudes, and motivations that prevent us from experiencing the freedom Saint Augustine spoke of.

Below are three models that can be used by teenagers or adults in making an examination of conscience. They are not strict methods; rather, they are guides that can be adapted as needed by the user. One person might prefer the traditional model and use it exclusively, and another might alternate between two or all three models.

Whichever model we follow, the goal of each examination is to help us identify the causes of our sinful actions and lead us to true repentance.

1. A Traditional Examination of Conscience Based on the Ten Commandments and the Five Precepts of the Church

Many books have been written, some poetic and others more practical, that teach us how to make a traditional examination of conscience by carefully reading the Ten Commandments and the Five Precepts of the Church and considering whether they have guided our decisions. This form has stood the test of time and continues to be of value to many people.

The Ten Commandments and the Precepts of the Church are essentially moral values that were presented in the language of norms or laws to make them understandable to all people. It is a mistake to focus on the *letter* of the law: we need to reflect on the *spirit* behind the law. For example, the first commandment says, "Have no other gods besides me." Thinking of the letter of the law, we might reply that we don't worship other gods; however, the spirit of the law invites us to think about what other values or persons have occupied the honored place that God alone should occupy in our life.

Keeping in mind this suggestion, read carefully each commandment and the questions that follow. Feel free to ask your own questions in addition to the ones provided. Asking them in the first person singular *(I)* will help you test the sincerity of your answer.

The Ten Commandments

1. You shall have no other gods before me.
- Is there something in my life more important than God?

- Are my possessions more important than my religious responsibilities?

2. You shall not take the name of the LORD your God in vain.
- Am I careful when I use God's name?
- Do I use inappropriate language when discussing religious topics?
- Does God truly guide my steps? How?

3. Remember to keep holy the LORD's Day.
- Do I honor the Lord's Day?
- Do I rest on the Lord's Day, or do I work when I really don't need to?

4. Honor your father and your mother.
- Do I respect my parents even when I disagree with them?
- Do I hurt my parents with words or actions?
- Do I stay in touch with them in spite of living far from them?
- Do I help them if they are in need?

5. You shall not kill.

- Do my actions and words show respect for life?
- Do I value my life and others' lives when I drive?
- Do I support the pro-life movement?
- Do I harbor bitterness or hatred toward another person? Whom?
- Am I violent?

6. You shall not commit adultery.

- Do I unnecessarily expose myself to photographs, images, or films that bring to mind impure thoughts?
- Do I control my eyes and my thoughts in the company of attractive people?
- Have I remained faithful to my spouse?
- Do I have friends who lead me to sin?

7. You shall not steal.

- Do I respect the possessions of others?
- Have I stolen something that is not mine? Did I return it?
- Have I violated the confidence of others?

- Have I spent money recklessly?
- If I am in a position of responsibility:
  Do I pay a just salary?
  Do I pay my bills?

8. You shall not bear false witness against your neighbor.

- Have I lied or exaggerated the truth of a situation to make others look bad?
- Have I told half-truths for personal gain?
- Have I spoken behind my friends' backs?
- Have I slandered others?

9. You shall not covet your neighbor's wife.

- Am I jealous of another couple's happiness?
- Am I respectful in my behavior and words when I'm with my friends' spouses?

10. You shall not covet your neighbor's goods.

- Do I envy the possessions of others?
- Am I bitter when another person has things I don't have?

Precepts of the Church

1. You shall attend Mass on Sundays and on holy days of obligation and rest from servile labor.

- Do I go to Mass each week?
- Am I alert and aware in Mass?
- Is the Mass central to my life?
- Do I skip Mass without a good reason?

2. You shall confess your sins and you shall receive the sacrament of the Eucharist at least during the Easter season.

- Do I try to grow through the sacrament of reconciliation, or have I grown lax in my participation?
- Do I regularly review my life, identifying actions and omissions that affect me and those around me?

3. You shall observe the days of fasting and abstinence established by the Church.

- Do I practice spiritual exercises and works of charity during Advent and Lent?

- Do I fast with the intention of opening my spirit more fully to things of God?

4. You shall participate in the Church's Mission.
- Do I participate in evangelization efforts and in service work in my parish or diocese?
- Am I concerned whether my actions and lifestyle draw others to Christ?

5. You shall help provide for the needs of the Church.
- Do I offer my time, talent, and treasures as an active Church member?
- Do I accept the responsibility of *being* the Church, not just *belonging to* the Church?

2. Examination of Conscience
Based on the Gospels

To follow this model, you must have time and be spiritually disposed, as during a retreat or on a day when you have at least several hours to pray. In this exercise you will review your life with the guidance of passages from chapters 5, 6, and 7 of Matthew's Gospel.

Some experts say these chapters of Saint Matthew synthesize Jesus' teachings. They reveal what Jesus means by the new law, for they speak about attitudes and not commands. The spiritual principles inspire wholeness and health.

Find a comfortable place to sit, then take a few minutes to quiet your thoughts. Imagine you are one of many people at the foot of the mountain listening to the Master. Imagine Jesus is speaking directly to you. Read the verses below, pausing to reflect on the questions provided or on your own questions as you review your life.

**"Blessed are the poor in spirit,
for theirs is the kingdom of heaven."**

- What does it mean for me to be poor in spirit at this time of my life?
- What sort of material dependencies prevent me from being poor in the way Jesus meant?

**"Blessed are those who mourn,
for they will be comforted."**

- What causes my sadness and preoccupations?
- How can I find God's consolation?

**"Blessed are the meek,
for they will inherit the earth."**

- Am I vain in how I dress or present myself?
- How can I publicly speak of my accomplishments and virtues without falling into vanity?

**"Blessed are those who hunger and thirst
for righteousness, for they will be filled."**

- Am I enthusiastic about living Christian ideals in my life? How?
- Do I support those who work hard or sacrifice comfort to make the world a better place?

**"Blessed are the merciful,
for they will receive mercy."**
- Do I share the pain of those who suffer?
- Am I doing anything to alleviate suffering and pain in our society?

**"Blessed are the pure in heart,
for they will see God."**
- Do I review the intentions of my actions?
- Do I consider the motivations behind my actions when personal gain will be the outcome?

**"Blessed are the peacemakers,
for they will be called children of God."**
- Do I work for peace? How?
- Do I believe in reasonable agreements to resolve problems before using force?

"Blessed are those who are persecuted for righteousness' sake, for theirs is the kingdom of heaven."

- Do I defend Christian values even when it may lead to a personal attack?
- Do I make fun of other Christians?
- Am I embarrassed to be known as a Catholic?

"You are the salt of the earth."

- Do I enrich the lives of others, or do I dishearten them?
- Am I aware of the mission God has given me to fulfill? What is that mission?

"You are the light of the world."

- Am I light or darkness?
- Do my life and Christian testimony encourage others in their journey of faith?
- How do I give this witness?

"You have heard that it was said 'You shall not murder'...but I say to you that if you are angry with a brother or sister..."

- Do I harbor hatred toward someone?
- Have I "killed" someone in my heart?
- Have I ignored someone in need of my attention?
- Do I wish the death of someone?
- Do I hate someone?

"You have heard that it was said, 'You shall not commit adultery'...but I say to you that everyone who looks at a woman with lust..."

- Do I enjoy looking at images that conjure up impure thoughts?
- Have I desired another person with disrespect?

"Let your word be 'Yes, Yes' or 'No, No.'

- Is there harmony among what I feel, think, and do?
- Am I sincere?
- Do I say things just for my own benefit?
- Do I lie?

**"You have heard that it was said,
'An eye for an eye and a tooth for a tooth.'
But I say to you, if anyone strikes you
on the right cheek, turn the other also."**

- Am I angry?
- Do I want vengeance?
- Am I violent?
- Do I impose my will on others?

**"You have heard that it was said, 'You shall
love your neighbor and hate your enemy.'
But I say to you, Love your enemies and
pray for those who persecute you."**

- Do I seek peace or revenge?
- Do I despise those who are not part of my life?
- Do I scorn people of other races, religions, or
  social classes?

**"When you give alms, do not let your left
hand know what your right hand is doing."**

- Are my acts of charity selfishly meant to
  help me get along with someone instead of
  performed selflessly?

- Do I have a sincere and generous heart?
- Do I value the needy and see them as my brothers and sisters, or do I think they are beneath me?

Continue reading until the end of chapter 7. In the future, consider reading chapters 10 through 13 of Saint Luke's Gospel, formulating your own reflection questions.

3. Examination of Conscience Based on Relationships With Others

Another way to make an examination of conscience is to reflect on your relationship with God, with yourself, with others, and with creation.

My relationship with God
- Is God the center of my life?
- What things or people rank higher on my scale of values than God?
- Is the Gospel a guide for my life?
- Do I make time for prayer? When?

- How important were my religious principles in the decisions I made this past week?

My relationship with myself
- Do I care for my body as I should, as befits a "temple of the Holy Spirit"?
- Do I feed my spirit with beneficial reading, television programs, and conversations?
- Do I take care of my health by watching what I eat, relaxing, and exercising?
- Do I avoid abusing alcohol, drugs, and other things that create an unhealthy dependency?
- Do I control my choices or do the Internet, telephone, or gambling control my life?

My relationship with my family
- As a son or daughter, do I respect the authority of my parents?
- Do I help them and have patience with them?
- Do I have a caring relationship with them?
- As a father or mother, do I give my children a good example?

- Do I discuss our child/children's education with my spouse?
- Do I help my brothers and sisters when they are in need?
- Do I enjoy family life and work so that our home has a healthy environment?
- Do I help keep the house clean and in order?
- Am I concerned with the welfare of my family or am I preoccupied with my personal agenda?

My relationship with other people

- Am I responsible at work?
- Do I help my coworkers or do I take advantage of them?
- Do I work hard when I'm on the job?
- Do I fulfill my responsibilities at work?
- Have I selfishly used others to help further my career?
- Am I responsible at school?
- Am I friendly and respectful with teachers and school officials?

- Do I finish my homework and give sufficient time to schoolwork?
- Do I try to maintain good friendships with my classmates?
- Do I avoid using drugs and stay clear of gangs?
- Do I respect my friends?
- Do I mock or make fun of the weaker students?
- Do I foster a relationship with the neighbors?
- Do I respect others' space and need for silence?
- Do I help keep the neighborhood clean, and do I clean up when others have littered?
- Do I take my friends' problems to heart?
- Do I vote for the most honest and capable people?
- Do I work for justice in the world?
- Do I support causes that defend the poor and the most vulnerable?

My relationship with creation

- Do I help care for the earth, our shared human home?
- Do I support organizations that work to protect the environment?
- Do I use products that damage the planet?
- Do I try to conserve energy in all its forms: electricity, natural gas, and gasoline?
- Do I throw trash on the street?
- Do I recycle?
- Do I buy unnecessary things?

The Sacrament of Reconciliation

When you have finished your examination of conscience, go to the confessional and ask forgiveness for your sins. Begin by expressing sincere repentance, and then confess your sins as they are, with no justifications.

The priest will suggest a penance, and then he will extend his hand over your head and say the words of absolution. Next, he will ask you to say an act of contrition. After you finish, he will send you forth in peace.

Later, you can complete the penance which, depending on your confession, may include returning something, asking forgiveness of someone, and/or performing a work of charity.

The goal of the sacrament of reconciliation is to help us focus our eyes on Jesus, our Lord and Redeemer. Because of him we are sons and daughters of God and can experience firsthand the grace shared with us at our baptism.

Confession as the Sacrament of Happiness

We have offered you three models for making a good examination of conscience in the hope that you will use them to you review your life and grow spiritually. Avoiding sin and choosing good are wonderful ways to improve human relationships and grow as a person. May God our Father fill you with his Spirit so you may live according to his will.

Act of Contrition

My God, I am sorry for my sins with all my heart. In choosing to do wrong and failing to do good, I have sinned against you whom I should love above all things. I firmly intend, with your help, to do penance, to sin no more, and to avoid whatever leads me to sin. Our Savior, Jesus Christ, suffered and died for us. In his name, my God, have mercy on me.